Hope in Community

Hope in Community

Reflections & actions for Holy Week & Easter

Ruth Harvey (Ed.)

wild goose publications

www.ionabooks.com

First published 2026 by
Wild Goose Publications
Suite 9, Fairfield
1048 Govan Road, Glasgow G51 4XS, Scotland
A division of Iona Community Trading CIC
Limited Company Reg. No. SC156678
www.ionabooks.com

ISBN 978-1-80432-411-0

Cover photo: Iona March 2025 © Simon Herbke

Printed in the UK by Bell & Bain, Thornliebank, Glasgow

FSC
www.fsc.org
MIX
Paper | Supporting responsible forestry
FSC® C007785

Contents

Introduction

Ruth Harvey

'The historic story of Christ, the outside story of Christ, suddenly emerges as the inside story of yourself – and it's this inner story, this inner parallel, that really makes the Bible inspired, so that to your condition it becomes the living word of God.'
George MacLeod[1]

Hope and love, hallmarks of the living word of God, root and inspire us. Hope is the 'condition' of the Iona Community in these days. Inspired by stories of Christ, and by testimonies of brave people of goodwill everywhere, we affirm that our faith is 'rooted in hope: lived in community'. This current theme underpinning our life in community refers to the determination, commitment and courage that is the essence of faith. This kind of hope is no fingers-crossed optimism. We believe, as seekers on the journey of faith, that the love and justice which we live out in our daily lives is transformative when it is joined with the love and justice of our neighbour in community; and when it is rooted in the love, justice, peace, truth and hope flowing through the Bible and other sacred texts.

This year we deliberately sought out, as our Holy Week and Easter writers, younger theologians: writers who are part of our Young Adults Group, or who have volunteered or lived with us recently in Community. In the flux of turbulence and uncertainty in our world, we are held strong, and galvanised to action for justice and peace by voices of wisdom, leading us from within our youth networks. Taking the Revised Common Lectionary as their starting point, each author has offered a reflection, a prayer or meditation, and a pointer to action.

The reflections offered here are an invitation to lean into the historic story of Christ, so to connect with the inner story by which we live. They are an invitation to encounter the full range of human emotions: anger, confusion and betrayal; fragile love, tender humility, deep joy. And in the end, they are a heart-wrenching plea: *'Turn me over, Jesus, ... back to the streets and alleyways until my love grows at least equal to my anger if not greater.'* In the face of raw anger, raging hurt, wild confusion, bitter betrayal, the invitation in these days is ultimately to love, to kindness, to hope: undervalued commodities in a world where 'commodity' has a human price, and 'value' drips from privilege.

The kind of hope to which the stories here beckon may not be a gentle hope. The *'gap between hope and fulfilment'* may taunt, may even breed despair. Or it may galvanise – point to possibility:

> *'And somewhere in the corner of our minds,*
> *suspicion flies to warn us that the gap between*
> *our hopes and their fulfilment is somewhat large –*
> *and slides away again.'*

Our writers here explore the 'feet-on-the-ground' gap between hope and fulfilment through the weaving of the outside story of Christ with their own. Each of these inspired authors knows what it means to live, rooted in hope, in community. Each has either shared *the common life commitment* through living with the Iona Community in intentional community at Iona Abbey; or has made an intentional *commitment to living our Rule of Life* as part of our scattered, global community. Some fit both of these categories! From a range of denominations and backgrounds, they dance in that gap between hope and fulfilment providing food for thought, nourishment for the soul and hope for the journey.

Sunday: Resurrection

I do not know
what resurrection is
(though I'm almost sure
it has something to do
with hallowing the common ground).
Of course, that's not all of it.

I expect one day I'll get up
and find that it sneaked up on me
while I wasn't looking,
and maybe even that it's been there all along.
That's as may be.
There's no point in trying to see things
before you are ready.
You have to walk before you can run.

In the meantime,
I believe in it.
And now it feels like an initial step.
For now,
it will do.
It is enough.

(Kathy Galloway)

Note:

1. All quotes taken from the 'Coming to Jerusalem' sequence of poems in *Love Burning Deep: Poems and Lyrics*, by Kathy Galloway, SPCK, 1993

Palm Sunday

Bible reading:

Matthew 21:1–11

'Tell the daughter of Zion,
Look, your king is coming to you,
humble and mounted on a donkey,
and on a colt, the foal of a donkey.'

The disciples went and did as Jesus had directed them; they brought the donkey and the colt and put their cloaks on them, and he sat on them. A very large crowd spread their cloaks on the road, and others cut branches from the trees and spread them on the road. The crowds that went ahead of him and that followed were shouting,

'Hosanna to the Son of David!
Blessed is the one who comes in the name of the Lord!
Hosanna in the highest heaven!'

Matthew 21:5–9, NRSVUE

Reflection:

This is one of the readings I think a lot of people know and one I look fondly back to from my childhood. It has been told so many different ways every year at Easter, so I feel a little daunted to take on a reflection. I will try my best.

I first tried *Lectio Divina* at Iona Abbey with some of the other volunteers and staff. It is a way to foster communication with God through contemplative practice. You read the passage through, usually one of scripture, and listen for a word or phrase that touches your heart. When I read this passage through in order to write this reflection one word jumped out at me so much it felt like it slapped me in the face. It felt like a moment of true connection to see this word laid out before me on the page.

What was the word? … Colt. The kind of donkey Jesus is to ride on into Jerusalem.

A colt is a young horse or donkey that is unbroken, hasn't been ridden before, still untamed and wild. You see the horse version a lot in cowboy movies; they are the ones bucking people off into fences for getting on their backs.

Meditation:

Find a quiet place. Close your eyes and imagine Jesus riding into Jerusalem on the young colt. Notice his gentleness. Ask yourself: what can I learn from Jesus choosing the colt? …

Recently I took some horse-riding lessons. These horses are the complete opposite of a colt. They are desensitised, patient, only sometimes a little stubborn. A horse is commonly known to have three speeds: walking, trotting and then cantering. I have learned that when a horse trots it already feels very, very fast and that it takes a lot more work than you think. You have to become one with the rhythm of the trot. Sometimes I was very relieved when the lesson ended as it was so exhausting to remember how to communicate and be confident with the horse. I cannot imagine ever getting on a colt. At least not willingly.

This could not have been a comfortable ride for Jesus. I can imagine it was not the smooth ride we normally picture. Why would he give purpose to this colt? It is such an important image for us, for Jesus to enter powerfully on the back of a donkey. But perhaps this is a lot more of a humble image than I first perceived. A foreshadowing image to a time in Jesus' life of hardship before the cross, one of endurance, one of hope. Before light comes darkness.

Action:

Palm Sunday stands between celebration and the cross. Light a candle and reflect on both joy and coming sorrow. Thank God that hope remains even when the road leads through suffering.

I wonder what Jesus was thinking, was he praying that he wouldn't fall off, like me in my horse-riding lessons? Was he hoping that the colt would keep going, as donkeys can be particularly stubborn? What does it mean for Jesus to be at one with the colt? Jesus of course knew what was to come; maybe he couldn't focus on riding as he entered his last week.

So as we enter this time of waiting, let us remember the light at the end of the tunnel.

Prayer:

God, help us when we are in the dark to look for light,
to have endurance to walk in the path of Jesus.
When we feel small or overlooked,
help us to see your purpose set for us.

Jesus, on Palm Sunday you entered Jerusalem
not with power and force but with humility.

You chose the difficult path to show us your love.
Help us to show that love to others and to you.

We place our hope in you.
Reign in our lives with mercy, humility and love.
Three in One, perfect in unity,
now and forever.
Amen.

Evie Nieboer

Monday of Holy Week

Bible reading:

John 12:1–11

Then Mary took about a pint of pure nard, an expensive perfume; she poured it on Jesus' feet and wiped his feet with her hair. And the house was filled with the fragrance of the perfume.

But one of his disciples, Judas Iscariot, who was later to betray him, objected, 'Why wasn't this perfume sold and the money given to the poor? It was worth a year's wages.' He did not say this because he cared about the poor but because he was a thief; as keeper of the money bag, he used to help himself to what was put into it.

'Leave her alone,' Jesus replied. 'It was intended that she should save this perfume for the day of my burial. You will always have the poor among you, but you will not always have me.'

John 12:3–8, NIV

Reflection: What's it worth?

The anointing at Bethany appears in all of the gospels. The scent of expensive perfume leaks from the pages of Jesus' life again and again. John's might be the most extravagant telling. He paints a picture of the reclining Lazarus, of Mary's hair on Jesus' feet, foreshadowing his imminent death. Jesus says, 'It was intended that she should save this perfume for the day of my burial.' As we enter Holy Week, that time is on the horizon.

Judas protests that in using her perfume, Mary is wasting it. He claims that the extravagance of her welcome, her show of love and service to Jesus when he enters her home, directly negatively affects the poor through an absence of giving. Yet, our author makes it clear that Judas' intentions come from a desire to get his grubby hands on the money.

We might first see this as the dichotomy: which would be a greater waste? For the perfume to change hands, again, and fill the shelves of a wealthy buyer, while Judas pockets the money? Or for the perfume to be spent? But Jesus doesn't dismiss Judas on the grounds that he cannot be trusted. He may well be aware of the man's self-interest, but what he actually dismisses is Judas' supposedly philanthropic suggestion. Why? Because the perfume is not being wasted. It is being used exactly as planned.

Jesus continues, 'You will always have the poor among you, but you will not always have me.' This has the potential to be a sticky passage. 'Stop worrying about the unwashed masses, these luxuries should be spent on me, the chosen one.' If this were the first section of the gospels one encountered, the impression given of Jesus might be of entitlement above all else. But, as always, context changes everything. Jesus' life is defined by his love of the unloved – the poor, the sick, the 'sinners'. So why not give every penny, every resource, to their care?

The value of perfume can be measured in two ways. There is financial value, a quantification Judas immediately jumps to, or sensory delight. The reason perfume is worth anything in the first place is because of its olfactory beauty. It can be used in ritual, to heighten certain experiences, and above all – for pleasure. Access to material pleasure is essentially why smelling good is a symbol of status in the first place. This is something we can so easily forget, skipping our creaturely sensory response to consider something purely for its surface cost.

Jesus, as always, is not concerned with wealth and status. He sees, in the perfume, not a means to an end. His care, his generosity, is not a bookkeeping exercise. When we try to follow his example in working for God's community on Earth, this fact should be a great relief, and a great promise.

An event took place in 1994 that I spend a lot of time thinking about. The KLF, a British band who experienced huge chart success, took themselves to the Isle of Jura and burned £1 million. They then went on a tour of the UK showing a film of the burning to live audiences, asking for help in figuring out why they did it. Pretty much everyone hated it. The main argument against the act? 'You should have done something charitable. What a waste.' I do not wish to argue for or against the moral value of their actions, relative to the money's other imagined potentialities. But I am fascinated by the author John Higgs' argument about it: that burning the money was the only way to deny its power. As Bill Drummond of the KLF acknowledged, they weren't using their money to make a statement about art, but using art to make a statement about money.[1] After all, the KLF did not destroy any resources other than little pieces of paper. There was still the same amount of food, shelter, labour, medicine in the world.

So why was everyone so angry about it? Because we have collectively agreed that money makes things happen. And we are trapped in a world in which, in so many ways, that is the reality. But sometimes, is it not useful to step outside our faithful, even idolatrous, trust of the stuff? Jesus says, 'You will always have the poor among you, but you will not always have me.' He is about to give up his life, but he does not give up Mary's perfume. The money from its sale could have been another positive drop in the ocean among many. But its use holds its own value, in sense and experience – and what better time to indulge than in one's final days on Earth?

Jesus' incarnation doesn't end poverty. Far from it: he acknowledges its systemic presence. This does not mean that we can stop working consistently to ease suffering and form community, trading it for luxurious hedonism in the everyday. But there is a place for extravagance, in giving and receiving. Directing our resources towards a full life is not as simple as imposing a kind of austerity, personal or societal.

The things and places that make me feel most alive are, from a perspective that quantifies financial and/or status-centric value, highly inefficient. In fact, they border on the practically ridiculous. They're festivals that build a city for a weekend. Classrooms that teach not correct answers to exams, but methods for artistic expression. A little island off an island on the West Coast of Scotland where it is highly inconvenient to run an abbey. Highly inconvenient to welcome guests from all over the world in all weathers. An island from which, on a clear day, you might get a glimpse of Jura.

Easter Sunday might be a day of celebration, but we're not there yet. In the final, dramatic days of Lent, we will lament the darkness. The tomb will be sealed shut. I urge, however, some expanded sense of what it means to be alive, even in full awareness that the future does contain great suffering. Our world, and our lives, are not all sunshine and roses because Jesus died. But if we see in these gospels any vision of divinity, to take away only an example of self-flagellation and penny-counting would be to ignore what's right there in the text. Smell the perfume. Give one another your most extravagant love. After all, we will not always have one another.

Blessing:

May you receive your daily bread
but may your garden blossom too.
May you not forget to look out of the window sometimes,
making tea
or worrying in a whirlwind of unknowns.

May you see the bright field
on your way to work
and hold it with you
throughout the mundane tasks
and the limitations of bodies and time.

Every once in a while
may you see everything all at once.

When you forget to stop for roses,
or when you can't, for a while
may their scent become unavoidable.

May your gifts be used
and guests come to share them.
The trials of the coming days
will be softened as long as it lingers,
that changed air.

Action:

Find two or three things in your house which smell great – perhaps perfume, a candle, incense or flowers. Take each item and spend five minutes focusing on its scent. How does it make you feel? Could you incorporate this into a daily ritual?

Give someone a gift for no reason other than the joy of it. It doesn't have to be expensive – you might also give time and effort. The key is to make their day more beautiful. Perhaps you could bake them something, draw them a picture, buy them a bunch of flowers. If you want to push this, you might offer the gift to a stranger: leave it on a train, keep it in your pocket for a queue conversation …

Write a prayer or poem of thanks for something that might be deemed 'inefficient' but which makes you feel more alive.

Indigo Maynard Watts

Note:

1. John Higgs, *The KLF: Chaos, Magic, and the Band Who Burned a Million Pounds*, Weidenfeld & Nicholson, 2012, pp. 237–8

Tuesday of Holy Week

Bible reading:

1 Corinthians 1:18–31

Consider your own call, brothers and sisters: not many of you were wise by human standards, not many were powerful, not many were of noble birth. But God chose what is foolish in the world to shame the wise; God chose what is weak in the world to shame the strong; God chose what is low and despised in the world, things that are not, to abolish things that are, so that no one might boast in the presence of God. In contrast, God is why you are in Christ Jesus, who became for us wisdom from God, and righteousness and sanctification and redemption, in order that, as it is written, 'Let the one who boasts, boast in the Lord.'

1 Corinthians 1:26–31, NRSVUE

Reflection: Seeing wisdom in the despised

Holy Week is a deliberate time of reflection for many, as we mark some of the final days of Jesus' life. Today the reading brings into focus the differences between human wisdom and God's wisdom, and presents the idea that God's wisdom is far beyond our understanding. And that in those we seek to exclude, we can find God. It calls us to accept that there will always be *something* beyond our understanding.

Lectio Divina is a method for engaging in and reflecting on (usually) biblical texts. The text is read multiple times, with those taking part invited to pick out a word or phrase that speaks to them. In reading 1 Corinthians 1:18–31 the phrase that stood out to us was 'the despised'. It made us ask the question – who are the despised? It is such a general term that this passage could be used to call for the inclusion of any group, but it is also specific enough to tell us something. It tells us that the people we least want to engage with, or be associated with, are exactly the ones we should be reaching out to.

To have 'the despised' is to have an 'other', which is to have an 'us' and a 'them'. The defining of an acceptable 'us' and an unacceptable 'them' is at the root of so many of the current discourses playing out in society.

From the stories of Jesus, it sounds like he was seen as an 'other' – a radical threat to the established order of things. His teachings are radical in that he calls us to reach out across human-made divisions and treat everyone as a neighbour. Jesus reaching out to those considered weak revealed the lack of wisdom of those in power; Jesus disregarded the fear of difference and provoked a fear in the powerful.

One such discourse that has thread its way through history is that around migration, and particularly those escaping hostile lands to seek asylum. The intensity of anti-migrant rhetoric has been building for some time, and it has somehow become a given that all sides of the political spectrum agree that immigration is bad. The lottery of geography, and therefore power, is not a fair one, so why should we exclude those who find the lands they call home engulfed in hostility? Many of the refugees that are being othered are fleeing from places because they've been othered to the point of violence or risk of violence. We must also remember Jesus himself was a refugee fleeing persecution by King Herod.

There are also those whose vulnerabilities are exploited by those who have more power, landing them on the wrong side of the law because they have been failed by systems meant to help those in need. They are often then branded as 'criminals', making access to meaningful employment even harder. And people who are unemployed or on benefits are branded as 'lazy' or 'free-loading'. While sex workers are denied rights given to other workers due to questions around the morality of their work.

And what do these groups have in common? Why do these groups make people uncomfortable? Each group challenges the status quo. They demonstrate the imbalances in our society, and by seeing these imbalances we are forced to acknowledge our privilege, and by nature our complicity. But isn't this exactly what Jesus spent his life doing? He reached out to those deemed as 'outcasts' or 'unclean'. In the end, Jesus himself became seen as such an outsider that he was deemed a threat to the status quo.

The jubilation of Palm Sunday morphed into public outcries against Jesus through a twisting of the narrative by those in power. Today we see this happening in the news, as statistics are manipulated, details are forgotten and context is ignored. But what the writer of 1 Corinthians is saying is to be wary of these stories. What we think of as wisdom may well turn out to be foolishness, and that those we 'other' are the ones God chooses.

And this is where we find hope. The power structures and divisions of humanity are what has othered so many people, and created an 'us and them' narrative. The passage is reminding us that this is not God's wisdom, but the perceived wisdom of the people in power. Therefore, our hope is that even though these people are despised now, that one day they will be welcomed, affirmed and included. And in it being our hope, it becomes our call to action to bring that day about.

Prayer:

God of all wisdom, we know that you truly understand what it is to be despised, turned against, and used as an easy scapegoat to hide injustice for those in power.

Open our eyes to witness such acts in our own communities and societies, and to truly see 'others' as fellow people.

Open our ears to the wise voices silenced by oppressive systems and the status quo, and especially when they call out our own privilege and complicity.

Open our mouths to speak truth to power, to challenge dangerous narratives with stories of humanity and hope.

Open our hands to offer hospitality, to say 'come on in, you are welcome'.

And open our hearts to all people, to invite conversation with acceptance, grace and humility, and to have our lives touched by diversity and wonder.

Amen.

Action:

Think about your local community: what group is currently seen as 'the other'? What would it look like to include that group more within your community?

What symbols could you use as a sign of welcome? How could you show these?

If you have felt 'othered', what has helped you to feel included?

Annie Sharples and Jack Woodruff

Spy Wednesday

Bible reading:

John 13:21–32

After saying this Jesus was troubled in spirit and declared, 'Very truly, I tell you, one of you will betray me.' The disciples looked at one another, uncertain of whom he was speaking. One of his disciples – the one whom Jesus loved – was reclining close to his heart; Simon Peter therefore motioned to him to ask Jesus of whom he was speaking. So while reclining next to Jesus, he asked him, 'Lord, who is it?' Jesus answered, 'It is the one to whom I give this piece of bread when I have dipped it in the dish.' So when he had dipped the piece of bread, he gave it to Judas son of Simon Iscariot. After he received the piece of bread, Satan entered into him. Jesus said to him, 'Do quickly what you are going to do.' Now no one knew why he said this to him. Some thought that, because Judas had the common purse, Jesus was telling him, 'Buy what we need for the festival,' or that he should give something to the poor. So, after receiving the piece of bread, he immediately went out. And it was night.

John 13:21–30, NRSVUE

Reflection: Playing the fool

We don't make much of April Fool's Day now, but in the Middle Ages, foolishness had an important place in the Church calendar, most of all at the 'Feast of Fools'. During this feast, a 'Lord of Misrule' – a peasant or lowly cleric – was chosen to become a mock Archbishop or Pope for a day. Mock-services would be held with all the roles reversed, a glimpse of revolution. For one day, the first really were made last, and the last made first.

In some ways, today's events seem very far from the raucous, revolutionary character of the Feast of Fools. Spy Wednesday is less a feast, and more a meditation on betrayal. It is sombre, and solemn, often marked by services held under the cover of deepening darkness, as candles are extinguished and congregants enter ever more into the mystery of Christ's suffering and death. Where is the foolishness here?

This year on Spy Wednesday, we hear John's account of Jesus' betrayal – which, a little confusingly, means we hear more of the same story tomorrow, on Maundy Thursday, from a different angle. On both days, we are invited to join Jesus at supper with his friends, and to watch the drama unfold. In today's Gospel reading, we zoom right in on that moment of crushing betrayal. Jesus knows what is to happen to him, and love and foreboding mingle as those he loves most deeply try to work out who among them is not who they seem to be.

The emotions that rise in me as I read John's telling of this scene are not unlike my feelings when watching the popular BBC reality show *The Traitors*. In the most intense scenes of the programme, an ever-dwindling group of 'faithfuls' try to sniff out the traitors in their midst, who are attempting to sabotage the game. As viewers, we know who the traitors are, and inevitably end up shouting at the screen when sure signs of dishonesty that seem obvious to us go unnoticed, often due to the strong friendships and alliances that the players form – or, the rivalries that cloud judgement and turn the faithful against one another.

Again and again, the faithful appear totally naive to the traitors' plotting, forgetting that they are hiding in plain sight. It is almost as though they do not want to believe that any of them could be a traitor; hardwired for connection, they cannot imagine that any of their fellow-contestants may not be all that they seem. As it is with *The Traitors*, so it is with Jesus' friends. They ask who the betrayer is among them, but do they really want to know? Perhaps for them it was easier to be wilfully foolish, determined not to see the incriminating passing of bread, or to hear Jesus' request for Judas to act quickly. It is difficult to believe that the disciples were really that oblivious. Love has made them foolish: even as Jesus unmasks Judas right in front of them, they cannot see him as a traitor. No one, John tells us, could understand what Jesus had done.

There is a sobering message here for those of us who spend time around churches. The bonds we form are deep; we come to see each other as family; love grows from our sense of common purpose, common world view, common ritual. Life in community is an utter joy, as we find ourselves challenged and changed by strangers who become siblings, bound together by the love of Christ. And yet, we know that our love can make us foolish. Abuse can happen under our noses. We can be pointed so clearly to our collective failings to protect those who are most vulnerable, and still choose not to see, made foolish by the power of the bonds we form, which bind us from sensing our siblings' capacity for deception. We must see the passing of bread. We must hear the cry for mercy. We must keep watch for those who slip into the night, overcome by the temptations of power and wealth that beget hatred and violence.

Where, then, do we find hope on this Spy Wednesday? How do we resist the kind of foolishness that makes us complicit with violence? Notice Jesus in our scene. He does not collude. He is at once full of love, and utterly clear about what is happening around him. He tells the truth, plainly, by his words and actions. He does not choose foolishness that refuses to see evil; he chooses the foolishness – in the eyes of a world bent on destructive power – that refuses to join in with evil. The events of the coming days see Jesus open his hands to suffering and death, unmasking violence and scorning the tools of oppression. We must keep watch with him, as darkness falls.

Prayer:

Lighten our darkness, we beseech thee, O Lord; and by thy great mercy defend us from all perils and dangers of this night; for the love of thy only Son, our Saviour, Jesus Christ. Amen.

The collect for aid against all perils from the Book of Common Prayer (1662)

Action:

Pay attention. If you are involved in any kind of church work or volunteering, is your safeguarding training up to date? Is there anything you could do to make sure that you are ready to respond well if something concerns you?

Let your yes be yes. Dishonesty can so easily creep into our day-to-day routines. What if you were to commit to radical honesty this coming Easter season? No excuses or white lies: there's a humility that comes from telling it how it is.

Resist. Judas got swept away by the promise of power. Where do you hold power? Where could you give up or share power for the sake of empowering others? Is there anywhere where power has caused you to act against your better judgement? Spend some time meditating on your own power and ask the Spirit to guide you as you seek to hold your power well.

Molly Boot

Maundy Thursday

Bible readings:

John 13:1–17, John 13:31b–35

Then he poured water into a basin and began to wash the disciples' feet and to wipe them with the towel that was tied around him. He came to Simon Peter, who said to him, 'Lord, are you going to wash my feet?' Jesus answered, 'You do not know now what I am doing, but later you will understand.' Peter said to him, 'You will never wash my feet.' Jesus answered, 'Unless I wash you, you have no share with me.' Simon Peter said to him, 'Lord, not my feet only but also my hands and my head!' …

After he had washed their feet, had put on his robe, and had reclined again, he said to them, 'Do you know what I have done to you? You call me Teacher and Lord, and you are right, for that is what I am. So if I, your Lord and Teacher, have washed your feet, you also ought to wash one another's feet.'

John 13:5–9; 12–14, NRSVUE

'I give you a new commandment, that you love one another. Just as I have loved you, you also should love one another. By this everyone will know that you are my disciples, if you have love for one another.'

John 13:34–35, NRSVUE

Reflection: 'Be gentle when you touch bread'

Holy Communion. The Eucharist. The Lord's Supper. Mass. A family meal. An elaborate ritual. A feast. A party. A foretaste of the heavenly banquet. A memorial of Christ. A fragment of grace. Food for the soul. Weekly. Daily. Monthly. Very rarely, if at all.

Those of us who belong to, or have belonged to, church communities will likely have experience of being united and divided by how we deal with bread and wine. I remember the anxiety, as a new Christian and a teenager, over working out whether or not I was allowed to take part as cubes of white bread and shot glasses (I thought) of wine were passed around, and everyone else seemed to know what they were supposed to do. I downed the non-alcoholic wine like a tequila shot, its sweet stickiness coating the roof of my mouth as I struggled not to spit it back out again.

Years later, as a priest, I keep my earthenware chalice and paten in the boot of my car: gifts from the Iona Community after I visited with some other young theologians to lead a Community Week. Designed more for large groups of pilgrims, they are, it has to be said, comically large for the home communions and small services I usually use them for in my little rural churches. And yet, there is something utterly precious about using this particular cup and plate for gatherings of all sizes.

The weight of them grounds me. The size of them reminds me that, when we share bread and wine, we are part of a community so much greater than ourselves. I am, of course, always reminded of my Iona Community siblings, breaking bread in every time and place, but also of the whole communion of saints who have done so, and will keep doing so, for all eternity.

On Maundy Thursday, the Church recalls, in a particular way, the events of the Last Supper. This is not Corpus Christi, the triumphant feast celebrating the gift of bread and wine that those of us of a more Catholic persuasion may be used to. On Maundy Thursday, we gather in the evening and break bread in the dark, knowing that deeper darkness lies ahead. There is a fragility to the feast. A total humility. There is nothing polished about this meal, and the tender messiness of it all is brought into stark relief as Jesus, during supper, draws himself up from where he is reclining, grabs a towel, and begins to wash his friends' feet.

Some of us may feel, if we have been attending church for a while, that we become quite comfortable with Communion. I doubt, however, that many of us will ever be wholly comfortable with having our feet washed. It is intimate, visceral in a way that, I find, totally unnerves me in the best possible way.

The first time I experienced foot-washing as part of a service, it was my bishop washing my feet before my ordination. I was, I must admit, absolutely dreading it. I did not want my bishop, whom I had only met very briefly in quite a formal interview setting, to touch my feet, let alone wash them. And yet, honestly, and to my complete surprise – it was one of the most profound spiritual experiences I have ever had. As she knelt to wash my feet, my bishop looked at me, right in the eyes, and said, 'Thank you for who you are.'

I wonder how deeply Simon Peter dreaded Jesus washing his feet, as he watched his Lord move around the table. If he wanted to recoil at the touch, so out of place, so messy, intimate and visceral. How he understood, as Jesus looked at him, right in the eyes: 'Unless I wash you, you have no share with me.'

On Maundy Thursday, we stand on the precipice of the most sacred of weekends. We give ourselves to the drama of what is to come, to Passion and cross and tomb. We choose, more than ever, to have a share with Jesus. We are invited to forget to be comfortable with the story that forms us: to hear it with fresh ears and open hearts. Maundy Thursday may be a memorial of the Last Supper, but it is also the first supper of its kind. Treat it as though you are hearing those words for the first time: 'This is my body. This is my blood.'

And if Communion feels all too familiar to you, let the washing of feet remind you of the strangeness of it all. The strangeness that our Lord comes to us in the most ordinary of things – in the messiness, the fleshiness of it all. Let him have a share with you, and let him lead you into all that is to come.

Poem:

Be gentle when you touch bread.
Let it not lie uncared for, unwanted.
So often bread is taken for granted.
There is such beauty in bread;
beauty of sun and soil,
beauty of patient toil.
Wind and sun have caressed it.
Christ often blessed it.
Be gentle when you touch bread.

Discovered next to a loaf of bread tucked in an alcove at Cartmel Priory, England

Action:

Listen. Margaret Rizza has written a beautiful setting of this poem. Find it on YouTube or your go-to music streaming service, and give it a listen. Perhaps spend some time with it, letting the words inspire your prayers, or lead you into some time of silent meditation.

Pay attention. Next time you go to a service where bread and wine are shared, take part as though it is the first time. Watch what people do with their hands; what posture they adopt. How do you move through this strange ritual? Is there anything disquieting about it? What about it sustains or comforts you?

Foot-washing. You may be attending a foot-washing service today. If you wouldn't attend a foot-washing service usually, you might like to find one! But if not: the next time you wash yourself, or someone else, treat it as prayer. Let yourself be surprised by the tenderness of what you are doing. Let God meet you there.

Molly Boot

Good Friday

Bible reading:

Psalm 22

My God, my God, why have you forsaken me?
Why are you so far from helping me,
from the words of my groaning?
O my God, I cry by day, but you do not answer;
and by night but find no rest.

Yet you are holy,
enthroned on the praises of Israel.
In you our ancestors trusted;
they trusted, and you delivered them.
To you they cried and were saved;
in you they trusted and were not put to shame.

Psalm 22:1–5, NRSVUE

Reflection:

In our fast-paced world the focus is always on the next thing. The next thing to buy, the next thing to do, the next place to visit. So fast paced that it is easy to forget to stop and look at what has *just* happened. Given Jesus' execution happened over 2000 years ago, we have the knowledge of what happens next. We know that today is not the end of the story, and we can so easily begin to focus on what happens next, rather than stopping to be present and to feel what has *just* happened.

Good Friday is the day we remember the trial and execution of the political activist, prophet and teacher Jesus Christ. It is hard to imagine the terror of Jesus' followers as they watched their leader, who for many had become a symbol of hope, being murdered by the occupying force. As the movement behind Jesus built, I am sure his followers were aware of the growing tension between him and the religious authorities, and the disruptive nature of some of Jesus' actions, but I doubt they would have imagined it could escalate so suddenly from the joyful entrance to Jerusalem to his death just days later. Hope was very much present on Palm Sunday, but was any of it remaining by Good Friday?

The events of Good Friday bring up feelings of despair, suffering and hurt. And in remembering this need, we are reminded that sometimes we need to let ourselves feel and really be present in the hurt and despair, before we can come out of that place with any hope. Good Friday is the day of hurt and despair, before the waiting and being present of Saturday, before the hope and resurrection of Sunday.

The cries of despair from the writer of Psalm 22 may have resonated with Jesus' followers on Good Friday; they certainly did with Jesus. The writer is crying out for help from a God who they feel has abandoned them. Some of their words certainly sound hopeless. Yet to cry out in the first place implies that on some level there may be some small amount of hope that some-thing or some-being or some-one is out there listening, and that maybe that means something might change.

But does the message of Psalm 22 lull us into complacency? In their despair, the Psalmist is crying out to God for help. But how would it read if we changed a few of the words:

My friends, my people, why have you forsaken me? Why are you so far from helping me, from the words of my groaning?

My people, I cry by day, but you do not answer; and by night, but find no rest.

The plea to fellow humans for help feels different to one aimed at God. We cannot absolve ourselves so easily from the responsibility of being the ones to help alleviate suffering. To hear someone cry out for help is often a call to action, a call to bring hope; even if that action is to be intentionally alongside someone who is suffering, for it may not be a suffering to be solved.

The words of Psalm 22 are perhaps best known as those Jesus cried out with when on the cross. They perhaps begin to capture the pain and despair he will have felt. This experience of the worst pain and despair that Jesus suffers may not always give hope to people in dire situations today, but it might help them feel understood, seen and held by a God who has been there too. Jesus is present with those in anguish, pain and despair because of what happens on Good Friday. In December 2023, Munther Isaac, a Palestinian pastor, author and theologian in the West Bank, shared an image of the Nativity where Jesus was not in a manger but in the pile of rubble. The image of Christ in the rubble provides a visual demonstration of God's presence amongst places of violence, pain and suffering.

So, as we mark this day when we confront the suffering of Jesus and are perhaps more aware of the suffering of our world, we must remember that the place of violence, pain and suffering is exactly where we can find solidarity, where we can find God, and where we can find hope.

Prayer:

Christ on the cross,
Christ in the rubble,
Christ in all suffering,
Christ with us always,

challenge us to hear your cries
in the voices of those who despair.
Embolden us to see your tears
on the faces of those in pain.

May all who need comfort
feel held in your nail-scarred hands.

May all who are able to,
journey alongside all who long for healing,
knowing they are travelling with you.
Amen.

Action:

What suffering have you been aware of lately that you could take the time to be present with today?

Annie Sharples and Jack Woodruff

Holy Saturday

Bible readings:

Job 14:1–14, John 19:38–42

'A mortal, born of woman, few of days and full of trouble,
comes up like a flower and withers,
flees like a shadow and does not last.'

Job 14:1–2, NRSVUE

'But mortals die and are laid low;
humans expire, and where are they?
As waters fail from a lake
and a river wastes away and dries up,
so mortals lie down and do not rise again;
until the heavens are no more, they will not awake
or be roused out of their sleep.'

Job 14:10–12, NRSVUE

They took the body of Jesus and wrapped it with the spices in linen cloths, according to the burial custom of the Jews. Now there was a garden in the place where he was crucified, and in the garden there was a new tomb in which no one had ever been laid. And so, because it was the Jewish day of Preparation and the tomb was nearby, they laid Jesus there.

John 19:40–42, NRSVUE

Reflection: Burying the body of God

You probably wouldn't believe me if you met me now, but I used to believe every word of the Bible to be literally true. I spent hundreds of pounds doing apologetics courses to learn how to 'prove' that it was historically, scientifically, and theologically true. Yet no matter how well you can defend an idea in theory, life tends to smash through our neat systems and nice ideas about God, about meaning, about suffering. The author of the *Chronicles of Narnia*, C.S. Lewis, wrote a book after the death of his wife, Joy Davidman, called *A Grief Observed*. In the book Lewis states that *'My idea of God is not a divine idea. It has to be shattered from time to time.'*[1] The first time I experienced this shattering of my ideas about God was when I ended up in hospital with stomach issues in my early twenties.

During my time in hospital I had the space to question the very literal and narrow views of scripture and God I had been given throughout my teens and early twenties. The first Sunday that I returned to church it felt like the floor fell out from underneath me. All the sure and steady ideas I had about the divine collapsed and I felt myself falling in to doubt. One of the first things that I questioned was the Bible. I remember going to my former pastor and saying that I didn't think that the Book of Job literally happened, but that I still found it beneficial because it is one of the oldest accounts exploring the question that haunts humanity: why do we suffer? His response was to tell me that 'if it didn't literally happen then it has no value'.

Viewing Job as an account of history makes it all too easy to skip Job's description of the human condition in the passage offered to us this Holy Saturday as 'few of days and full of trouble' and to proceed immediately to the epilogue in chapter 42 where Job's fortune is restored, his livestock returned, he ends up with more children, and the passage says 'the Lord blessed the latter days of Job more than his beginning'. The all-too-common interpretation here is to say that the suffering was all worth it, as if new children erase the memory of those who died, as if friends showing up when things were going well made Job forget their absence in the middle of loss, as if God's justification in the story is satisfactory. From chapter 38 through to chapter 41, God, the Creator of the universe, essentially says, 'Job, you're not God.' Well, no shit, Sherlock, we have just read 37 chapters making that exact point and we hear the same conclusion in today's reading: 'mortals lie down and do not rise again'.

Job is uncomfortable reading for many of us because when we enter the story and begin to see our sufferings reflected in Job's it becomes glaringly obvious that the book does not have a satisfying ending. The whole story is tainted by the fact that everything that has happened to Job seems to have occurred because of a divine bet (Job 1:8–12). Job's friends come across as unhelpful idiots for even trying to explain suffering, as if reason heals the broken-hearted. They dismiss Job's suffering, telling him to just trust God (Job 8:5–6), they blame Job for the suffering, telling him his questions are sinful, and he must be guilty (Job 15:5–6), and they appeal to mystery, saying to Job, 'Can you fathom the mysteries of God? Can you probe the limits of the Almighty?' (Job 11:7). Last year my wife, Katy, sadly had two miscarriages and any time someone told her 'at least you know you can get pregnant' I found myself thinking of Job's frustration with Eliphaz, Bildad, and Zophar and their responses.

Like Job, we find ourselves in a world full of people offering confident answers about our suffering without ever daring to step into it with us in solidarity. It's easier to say 'just have faith' than it is to say, 'how long, O Lord?'. It's easier to blame the victim of suffering than it is to open ourselves up to the endless heartbreak found on the other side of compassion. It is easier to read Job as a story of faith where it all works out in the end, rather than a tale of unnecessary suffering, with questionable companions, and an unsatisfying conclusion. Just like it is easier to skip Holy Saturday in our Easter readings and jump ahead to the Resurrection. Because for many people the Christian story has become a story of endless optimism and Jesus has been transformed into a *'metaphysical Easter bunny ... a miracle weapon in service of the mighty'*.[2]

The invitation of Job, and of Holy Saturday, is to bury the body of God. Last year my Dad, Tom Gibson, died from dementia at the age of 66. There's this strange thing that happens when someone close to us dies; for weeks, maybe even months after their death we find ourselves forgetting. Forgetting that they have actually died. There have been many times in the last few months when I have found myself thinking, 'I should go and visit Dad soon.' Whenever that happens my mind takes me back to sitting in the funeral directors with my Dad, cold, embalmed, and lifeless. The memory of being physically with him in death made the loss that much more real and tangible but also final. Our reading from the Gospel of John describes for us the experience of those who were with Jesus' dead body and who buried him. A moment of finality when Job's expression 'mortals lie down and do not rise again' becomes real to us. God is dead, his body buried, and we mortals don't have the benefit of knowing whether resurrection is a sure bet for our hope.

In many ways for most of us, our lives are lived in a perpetual Holy Saturday. We exist between what feels like a divine bet and a divine justification for our few days that are full of trouble. Part of the beauty of the Christian tradition is that we are invited not to skip ahead to Resurrection Sunday, or to justify suffering with false hope of blessings in this life. Rather we are invited to sit at the tomb, maybe even to descend into hell with the incarnate one. Our faith does not ask us to avoid, dismiss, or skip over suffering as a minor inconvenience in a world where all things work together for good. It does however call us to face our suffering head-on, to bury the body of God not knowing if resurrection will ever occur, and as we confront the fragility of our lives to find ourselves surprised by the flowers in the garden surrounding our tombs. To see the beauty in the brokenness, to find peace in the midst of chaos, and to see goodness in unexpected places. Because we do not need optimism, we need hope, and hope is a radical act of seeing the divine at work even in the midst of death.

Prayer:

Jesus,
you descended into death and in so doing participated fully in our humanity.

When we can't imagine a way forward,
when life and hope seem absent from our circumstances,
be with us.

May we not avoid our suffering or pain
but instead cultivate within us the ability to face our experiences with honesty and with clarity.

As we journey through the valley of the shadow of death,
journey with us.
When our hearts are broken,
be near.

Like a flower that withers and a shadow that fades
may we be able to see beauty
even in the midst of our fragile lives.

May we sit long enough in the graveyard to be able to see
the garden that surrounds us.
Amen.

Action:

Spend some time today meditating on a loss or a recent experience of grief. Either write a person's name on a bit of paper, find an item which reminds you of a particular moment, or light a candle. In the presence of the name, item or candle use the above prayer and/or take 5-10 minutes in silence remembering your loss or grief.

Reach out. If you know someone who has recently experienced loss or is currently suffering, then make contact with them. I would suggest that instead of emailing or messaging them that you write a letter; this could be handwritten or typed/printed.

If you are able, take some time today to visit a loved one's grave or final resting place. Feel free to use the above prayer and/or take 5-10 minutes in silence remembering that person.

Read Job chapters 38 to 41 and consider God's response to Job's suffering. Write a letter to God in response. Consider: do you find God's answer satisfactory? Are you angry with God? How does Jesus' death affect your understanding of suffering? This response could be handwritten, typed/printed, or it could be a voice recording.

William Gibson

Notes:

1. C. S. Lewis (N.W. Clerk), *A Grief Observed*, Faber and Faber, 1961

2. Dorothee Sölle, 'Christofascism', in *The Window of Vulnerability: A Political Spirituality*, Fortress Press, 1990, p.140

Easter Sunday

Bible readings:

Colossians 3:1–4, John 20:1–18

Set your minds on the things that are above, not on the things that are on earth, for you have died, and your life is hidden with Christ in God. When Christ who is your life is revealed, then you also will be revealed with him in glory.

Colossians 3:2–4, NRSVUE

But Mary stood weeping outside the tomb. As she wept, she bent over to look into the tomb, and she saw two angels in white sitting where the body of Jesus had been lying, one at the head and the other at the feet. They said to her, 'Woman, why are you weeping?' She said to them, 'They have taken away my Lord, and I do not know where they have laid him.' When she had said this, she turned around and saw Jesus standing there, but she did not know that it was Jesus. Jesus said to her, 'Woman, why are you weeping? Whom are you looking for?' Supposing him to be the gardener, she said to him, 'Sir, if you have carried him away, tell me where you have laid him, and I will take him away.' Jesus said to her, 'Mary!' She turned and said to him in Hebrew, 'Rabbouni!' (which means Teacher). Jesus said to her, 'Do not touch me, because I have not yet ascended to the Father. But go to my brothers and say to them, "I am ascending to my Father and your Father, to my God and your God."'

John 20:11–17, NRSVUE

Reflection:

Weeping in despair, Mary Magdalene set her gaze on the empty tomb. I am always touched by her exclaiming that they have taken 'my Lord' away, conveying familiarity and depth of relationship. We can presume that Mary went to the tomb early to be near to Jesus and to mourn. She was so consumed with grief, or perhaps anger, over Jesus' body being humiliated again by being stolen, she did not notice her surroundings or recognise Jesus. As recorded in the Gospel of John, Jesus did not appear to Mary in spectacular glory but as a gardener. What a curiosity that the resurrected Christ appeared as a gardener. But of course what could be a more fitting image to honour the new creation?

'Do not hold on to me,' Jesus said to Mary, 'for I have not ascended to the Father.' Was Jesus here pushing Mary away? Dismissing her despair and joy? If Jesus was so concerned about his next move upwards why would he appear in such an approachable manner?

I spent quite a while wrestling with this. I wonder if the reason that Jesus gave, about his ascension, was not given to draw Mary's attention to where he would be going, but instead to reground Mary's attention to where she needed to be. Jesus did not want Mary to 'set her heart on things above', to cling to the glorified Christ, but to re-ground herself in the work of Christ her gardener. Maybe we see Jesus here reminding her that her faith and work would move on that place, and that she had a mission to go and share the blessing of seeing the resurrected Christ with the disciples.

As tempting as it might be to remove ourselves from 'earthly things' – perhaps like the those in power who are unwilling to recognise the climate catastrophe and to combat it as it needs – we are called to instead 'go' and 'tell them'.

I recently heard a sermon from Gethin Jones, a preacher in the ecumenical church that I grew up in in Cardiff. Gethin told us a story about the faith of Gwen. Gwen, he told us, religiously attends the weekly Bible study sessions run by the Church in Wales parish church where Gethin has retired to. Gethin commented that Gwen does not usually say very much, and anything she does say is prefaced with 'I'm probably wrong,' or 'I don't really have anything intelligent to contribute.' Gethin said that Gwen's contributions are always helpful and thought-provoking though; but he was especially struck by one story that she uncharacteristically told one week. Gwen, in a very matter-of-fact way, told the Bible study group that God had told her to go and see the diocesan Bishop to deliver a message. She went to the Bishop's house and he answered the door, saying, 'I knew you were coming.' And that was the story. Gwen had never met the Bishop before, nor did she spill the details of God's message. Gwen's faith was to trust God entirely. Just as Mary, in all the surprise, disbelief and overwhelming emotion, heard Jesus and went, Gwen heard God and just went.

Concentrating our hearts and minds on things above, rather than on earthly things, then, cannot possibly mean to disregard the earthly priorities of Jesus and his call to us to 'go'. I think, instead, we are to not remove ourselves from earthly things but from earthly agendas. To be a disciple of the resurrected Christ is to be rooted in hope. It is to follow Mary and Gwen who did not consider social doubts.

'What will people think when I tell them the man they have literally just seen crucified has appeared to me?'

'What on earth will the Bishop think with little old me turning up at his door?'

It is to trust Christ in community and to expect the Holy Spirit to already be where we are going. To trust in things above is to trust in the transformative power of life after death, cultivated by the presence of the Holy Spirit constantly renewing our world now, here, today. We are not called to remain weeping at the foot of the cross, consumed with our doubts and pessimism, but to be refreshed towards our ministry of cultivating, mending and repairing our world. To go and tell of our hope rooted in the Risen Lord.

It is especially in the times where the world outside the tomb feels as dark as inside the tomb, those times when withdrawal or hopelessness is so tempting, that we need to reorientate ourselves towards the Risen Christ. Our Christ who overcame death and prioritised returning to the little shoots and connecting again his community.

We are called to go and witness to the grace of our God who sacrificed their only Son and rose again in glory for our (our=all) salvation. Setting our hearts on Christ is setting our hearts on God incarnate, who even in the glorified, resurrected body – 'Christ is risen' – was the One closest to earthly things.

Prayer:

Resurrected Christ,
Gardener, Cultivator, Creator,
we rejoice on this Easter Sunday
in the boundless blessings
that touch each one of us
and renew every part of our world.

We pledge to you that
we will 'go'
and tell of your wonder,
and tend your Garden.

Risen Christ,
remind us of our hope of new life
as we commit ourselves to your work of repair.
Amen.

Action:

Record moments of hope to keep for yourself for when you are feeling overwhelmed in those moments of despair. Have you experienced a moment of trust and connection like Gwen? Have you been overwhelmed with awe and wonder like Mary – and felt a compulsion to go and tell? Have you seen fresh shoots grown and communities reconnect? Where? Have these as a gift to yourself for those days when the light does not seem brighter outside of the tomb.

Explore your heart and ask if you are doubting a calling from God. No matter how small the action, where is God asking you to go and tell?

On this Easter Sunday, what action could you do to help cultivate renewal in the world? Could you be carbon neutral for the day? How could you connect with others and help to build community?

Victoria Turner

Easter Sunday Evening

Bible readings:

Isaiah 25:6–9, Psalm 114, 1 Corinthians 5:6b–8, Luke 24:13–49

'Were not our hearts burning within us?'

Luke 24:32, NRSVUE

'I am sending upon you what my Father promised, so stay here in the city until you have been clothed with power from on high.'

Luke 24:49, NRSVUE

And he will destroy on this mountain
the shroud that is cast over all peoples,
the covering that is spread over all nations …

Isaiah 25:7, NRSVUE

Therefore, let us celebrate the festival, not with the old yeast, the yeast of malice and evil, but with the unleavened bread of sincerity and truth.

1 Corinthians 5:8, NRSVUE

Reflection: Unveiling the Kin(g)dom

The Kin(g)dom of God was revealed to me in community. A foundation had been set by my Roman Catholic upbringing and my involvement with the university chaplaincy, but it was in belonging to the L'Arche-inspired Lyn's House community that something of God was powerfully revealed – so much so that it changed the trajectory of my life.

Here, among this mixed-ability community of thirty or so, I found deep wells of joy made deeper by the ability to hold pain and grief. Here I found a culture of receiving and celebrating each individual for the generous God-crafted gift they are. Here – in laughter and in tears – here – applauding Mr Blobby dances, PhD completions, and songs on moose and juice – here – gathered by the dappled light under the bunting-draped cherry tree eating probably too many sugary snacks – here – sharing in life's simplicity as friends through weekly rhythms of shared meals and prayer. Here – I found my soul vivified, reverberating with the resonances of something True. Here – I found the Kin(g)dom of God.

Found? It was more like an unveiling; a gradual clearing of the mist of my worldly formation, enabling more of God's warmth and light to pierce through, extending the reaches of my spiritual sight to deeper horizons. God was no longer simply the being I was in personal relationship with, nor simply the being who also resided in all created beings whom I had a duty to love. But God was tangibly present in the dynamic web of love, joy, and right relationship itself. Drawing on the Quaker metaphor of 'inner light', I not only saw nodes of light residing in each individual life, but saw these as woven together by glowing beams of relationship, creating a splendid dome radiating the brilliance of the Kin(g)dom come. The Kin(g)dom made manifest by our choice to live into our full created and creative potential for relationship – with self, others, creation, and God. It is fitting that much of this unveiling of the Kin(g)dom happened in the Lyn's House community garden wherein an engraved sculpture reads *'It is only with the heart that one can see rightly; what is essential is invisible to the eye.'*[1]

Oh, the heart. I love the mention of the heart in today's gospel reading, which also speaks so poignantly to the dynamics of God being unveiled among us. Amid the fluctuation of sight being withheld and granted, and doubting minds being opened, it is the heart which is uplifted as a steadfast centre of knowing: 'Were not our hearts burning within us?' Though the journeying disciples only verbally articulated this once Jesus was revealed to them more obviously, their hearts still knew they were in the presence of God before their eyes and mind did. Similarly, the gathered group of disciples in Jerusalem felt noteworthy joy at the presence of Jesus among them, though their minds remained disbelieving and wondering. The presence of God animates our being, even though our eyes and minds might not recognise this as so.

This animation is energised and powerful. It led the disciples to make a seven-mile trek all the way to Jerusalem, in the dark, having only just arrived at their Emmaus destination! The Good News of Jesus being among them is too big to contain just the two of them. It is a revelation which begs to be shared in community. And not only shared, but witnessed to in community, as later and ultimately made possible by being 'clothed with power from on high'.

First guided to Lyn's House by a burning heart, I have since had the privilege of feeling my heart repeatedly burn within me through the witness of several intentional Christian communities across the UK, including the residential Iona Community. The presence of God is by no means exclusively unveiled in these contexts, but those who have experienced the Iona Community and/or other intentional communities, can probably attest to the quality of relationship – with self, others, creation and God – which thins the veil of our earthly formation to reveal more of the Kin(g)dom. To paraphrase from today's scriptures, something of 'the shroud that enfolds all peoples, the sheet that covers all nations is destroyed' and 'the yeast of malice and evil' is replaced with 'sincerity and truth'.

As evidenced by the story of the journey to Emmaus (among others), God retains the power to reveal Godself in quite dramatic ways. But we are also invited to participate in God's revelation; as the disciples did by noticing their burning hearts and letting themselves be animated into spreading the Good News. I believe a key part of this participation is living into the fullness of relationship God intended for us. In doing so, something of God is made tangibly present in ways which can be felt; as if something of the very fabric of God was woven by our relationships. I have consistently experienced intentional Christian communities, of the likes of Lyn's House and Iona, to beautifully embody what it means to live into this fullness of relationship, their witness as communities, rooted in attentiveness to the Spirit, powerfully thinning the veil and amplifying the felt-presence and dynamic activity of God for those among them and beyond. Praise be to God, who lives and breathes among and through us!

Prayer:

God of unveiling,
You reveal Yourself to us.

God of broken body breaking bread,
You invite us into relationship with You, Your people, and Your creation.

God of walking alongside,
You are among us always.

May we know these Truths deeply in our hearts,

and with Your help incarnate them,
that Your Presence might be felt vividly among us
and all around us,
making manifest Your ways.

Amen.

Action:

Draw an outline of your/a human body. Annotate it and colour it in to depict where and how you feel the presence of God in your body.

Journal or write a poem on how you experience 'God among us'.

Make a timeline of your life, marking moments when your heart burned within you. What do you notice? What followed from these moments?

Spaciously fill a page of paper with named stick figures of the significant people in your life.

By each person, write a word or sentence indicating that of God you experience(d) revealed through them/your relationship with them. If possible, share these insights with them. (This exercise can also be done in community, with everyone taking the time to reflect on the members of the community, followed by a time of sharing insights in community.)

Lakshmi Piette Walker

Note:

1. Antoine de Saint-Exupéry, *The Little Prince*, Reynal & Hitchcock, 1943

About the Contributors

Molly Boot: Molly (they/them) is a theologian, musician and priest, currently based in rural Gloucestershire. They're very enthusiastic about a lot of things, including music, prayer, LGBTQ+ liberation, and the stranger corners of medieval church history.

William Gibson is an Iona Community member, 2nd year candidate for ministry in the Church of Scotland, and 2nd year PhD student at the University of Glasgow, researching modern Scottish Church history. Previously William worked for the Student Christian Movement, and before that, during his time working at Apple, was part of leading unionising efforts in the first unionised Apple store in the UK.

Ruth Harvey is the Leader of the Iona Community.

Indigo Maynard Watts volunteered in the Programme Team at Iona Abbey in 2025, and is a new addition to the Iona Young Adults Group. She lives in Gloucestershire, and will generally be found writing about festivals and counterculture, or making colourful artwork.

Evie Nieboer: 'I'm Evie, 24, from Paisley in Scotland now living in Ghent, Belgium, with my husband Paul, whom I met on Iona, and son Theodore, who was born in August 2025. I volunteered at the Abbey for a few years and went on to be a part of the Resident Team in 2023. I am now an associate on the Iona Community's New Members Programme and co-convenor of the Young Adults Group.'

Lakshmi Piette Walker is passionate about intentional Christian community and the ways shared life bears witness to the presence of the living God. She is host of the Dwelling Place podcast and blog and author of *Dwelling Places: The Practice and Witness of Intentional Christian Communities* (SCM Press). She lives in rural Cumbria, where she is part of the emerging Rose Community, and can daily be found gallivanting through fields and woodland, relishing the groundedness of natural being and the dances of the wind.

Annie Sharples lives in Sheffield and enjoys spending time outside or reading with a big mug of tea. She is a Methodist and in the second year of the Iona Community's New Members programme. Annie is passionate about quiet activism, and is a trustee for the Fellowship of Reconciliation. She works for the JustMoney Movement, and has previously worked with the Joint Public Issues Team (JPIT) and in the Abbey kitchen on Iona.

Victoria Turner is the Director of Studies at the Scottish Episcopal Institute (Edinburgh). She is in the second year of the Iona Community's New Members programme and is a member of the United Reformed Church. Her PhD (2023), which explored the mission of the Iona Community and the Council for World Mission, will soon be published by Brill, and her other publications, including anthologies of talented young theologians (some of whom are Iona Community members), are published by SCM Press.

Jack Woodruff is a mathematician based in Sheffield, and in the second year of the Iona Community's New Members programme as well as being part of the Young Adults Group. Jack previously spent two seasons living and working on Iona at the Abbey, mainly in Housekeeping. He is also a Methodist and a regular pilgrim on Northern Leg of Pilgrim Cross.

Sources and acknowledgements